Something to Give

A Story for Families

Something to Give

A Story for Families

Written by
Naomi Stevens Smith

Illustrated by
Lari Taylor Smith

BONNEVILLE BOOKS
An imprint of Cedar Fort, Inc.
Springville, Utah

ISBN 13: 978-1-4621-3968-2

Published by Bonneville Books, an imprint of Cedar Fort, Inc.
2373 W. 700 S., Springville, UT, 84663
Distributed by Cedar Fort, Inc., www.cedarfort.com

Cover design by Shawnda T. Craig

Printed in the United States of America

10 9 8 7 6 5 4 3 2 1

Printed on acid-free paper

Acknowledgments

I am grateful for a good family—a grandmother who read me Bible stories when I was very young, Daddy and Mom with whom we took turns reading aloud from the scriptures as we sat around a blazing fire on cold winter nights in our little mountain town. The fire furnished the light for us as well as warmth because we could not always buy oil for our lamps.

I'm grateful to young brothers and sisters—all ten of them—who wanted stories and listened intently to "big sister." I am also grateful to my children who asked for stories at nap time.

I appreciate the help and encouragement of friendly publishers, and I'm most grateful to Lari, who did the illustrations, and to Marilyn, who helped prepare the manuscript for submission.

I dedicate this book to the dear families who have and do brighten my life.

An account of the miraculous feeding of five thousand people with five barley loaves and two small fishes. Told from the point of view of a hungry child who found that he did indeed have "Something to Give."

The Master said, "It is better to give than to receive."
I wonder, could that be true?
I'll share my shells with my sisters,
Paint more gourds for Samuel, too.
But I long for something to give to the Master!
Whatever could that be?
Worthy of one so noble and great—
From a poor shepherd boy like me?

Part 1

The sun, almost overhead, was still gently, wonderfully penetrating. Timothy dug his toes into the sand, savoring its heat and remembering days not too long past when his toes had sought the warmth of his body; days when he sat with knees hugged under his chin and cloak wrapped tightly about him.

An abundance of green grass grew between the stones on the hillside and spread like a lush blanket over the meadow below and the distant mountainside. The branches of the fig tree were swollen with leaf buds; the figs were larger than his thumb. In a few weeks they would no longer be hard and wooden to the taste. He could close his eyes and almost feel the tender flesh of a ripe fig in his mouth, the taste of the sweet warm fruit on his tongue, and the small seeds that broke with a pop when he bit them. Ah, a thing of joy and wonder was the ripened fig—and very tasteless and uninviting indeed, the green ones now above his head.

Today it was enough that he was here in his favorite spot. The sun was warm and delicious to his very bones, and the sheep were grazing docilely with no intent to stray. When the sun was high and the fig tree's shadow small, he could eat the fragrant barley loaves his mother had sent with him that morning. Not before midday must he eat; this he had learned well. When he ate too soon, the afternoon was unbearably long, and his stomach knew that hungry gnawing before the twilight hour when the sheep could be returned to the fold.

He raised the linen cover of his small basket and feasted his eyes on the plump brown loaves. There were five of them, fresh baked the evening before, and there were fish. His mother had risen early to roast them for him. He was hungry. The sight of food and its aroma tantalized him.

Ah! There was something more in the basket—something he had not thought to find—a wedge, nay, a full quarter of the little white cheese that had been sitting for three day's past on the shelf to ripen. It was the first to be made since the brown goat gave birth to her two spotted kids. Timothy had thought it would be placed uncut in the larger basket his father and uncles carried with them on the fishing boat.

Did this mean that his mother looked upon him no longer as a small child but as a man to share the cheese equally with his father and two uncles? He envisioned himself taking his evening meal with the men, heard himself telling of the day's happenings, while his father and uncles looked up from their food to listen.

It was true that his time with the sheep offered little to speak about. The days went by with small change in activity and no excitement. But had not David of old been a shepherd? He often thought of David when his ego suffered. But David had been a lad of broad shoulders, strong arms and sinew. It was known to all that he had often fought wild beasts to protect his father's flock. Woefully, Timothy regarded his own slender arms and legs. His father had called the frail limbs "spindles" in jest, to be sure. Nevertheless, it seemed certain that his arms and shoulders could not develop strength to draw in the fishing nets from the sea. Better he tend the few sheep from whose wool his mother made blankets and clothing. Timothy's father patted his son's head kindly as he did the two younger sisters. But there was not the light in his eyes that Timothy had observed at times when he looked upon Samuel.

Samuel, five years his junior, already showed promise of developing into a man of brawn and sinew, a son who could help his father control the fishing boat on the stormy Galilee and heft a net laden with fish. That it must be Samuel, instead of himself, to fulfill his father's hopes in a son was cause of much sorrow to Timothy. Was he not the firstborn? Was it not his birthright to follow in his father's footsteps? Often he knew a feeling of dark ugliness inside. Out of his wretchedness he built dreams of heroic deeds he must do that his father might know of his bravery and look upon him with pride. In his dreams he fought monsters for the safety of his father's sheep, even as David had done.

He turned his attention again to the basket of food and folded the linen carefully over the barley loaves. But the cheese he raised to his nostrils. The smell, so mellow and rich, was more than he could bear. This he would eat now.

He had no plan for sleep when he spread his cloak. He wanted only to stretch himself upon it while his body drank in the sun's warmth and he savored the goodness of the cheese. A good shepherd was always alert to the safety of his flock. Only a few weeks before, one of the older ewes had stepped in a hole and hurt her leg. He had bound it with linen from his basket. When he took the sheep to the well to drink, he had held back the others so that the ewe might not be crowded out. Then last season there had been the two newborn lambs whose mother had sickened and died. They had been so small and weak! He had fed them milk from a gourd until they were old enough to graze, and had known a warm feeling inside when they nuzzled close against him seeking love and care. Now, fully grown, they still ran to meet him each morning. Though it gave him pleasure, he could not speak of these things to his father and uncles. They were the gentle feelings and tasks a woman might know, not the strong courageous deeds of a man.

The soft, white cloud changed in form as it drifted across the sky. Drowsiness crept upon him so slowly and so insistently that when, from the brink of sleep, he struggled to put himself upon his feet, he was quite powerless to do so.

From the depths of his slumber he heard the tumult. But the sound of voices seemed only to be those of the crowd of people acclaiming him a brave lad. In his dream he had killed a fierce lion and brought it down from the mountain. As he awoke, he knew it to be only another dream and thought to find himself at home with his brother and sisters shouting at their play.

The sun had traveled across the sky. Its rays were no longer gentle. With stiff fingers he was gathering up his cloak to shake the dust from it when he realized that the voices had not been dreamed nor imagined. They were real and not too far away. The sounds came from the way of the sea, yet they were not the sounds of fishermen at work. Curiosity gripped him. Still clutching his cloak and basket, he climbed a small summit where he could view the sea and a long stretch of shoreline. Here he stopped and looked in astonishment. He shook his head violently lest he still be dreaming. He stared in disbelief.

Never had his eyes beheld so many people. As far as he could see they came along the shore—hundreds of them—walking in pairs, in groups, or singly. Some hurried on ahead to seat themselves on the grassy slopes of the adjacent mountainside, where already there was a large gathering. Others walked more slowly, some laboriously making their way. Six men were carrying a litter upon which was stretched a seventh. They were hurrying despite the load.

Anchored off the shore, a fishing boat swayed gently on the blue sea. It was not unlike the boat his father used, but where were the fishermen? And what could have brought so many people to this desert place? He could not turn back to his duties without knowing, not even if a vicious lion should choose this very moment to fall upon his sheep, which he noted were grazing undisturbed.

He moved toward the group on the mountainside. The men with the litter joined the others now. They did not seat themselves but were making their way through the multitude. Timothy felt that he must burst if he couldn't follow and see what they did. He ran faster over the rocky slopes. Many were joining the crowd but he was able to thread his slight form through them until he came straightway upon what he was seeking.

Never had his eyes beheld so many people.
As far as he could see they came along the shore.

The litter lay upon the ground, a little apart from the multitude, and it was empty. Beside it a frail, stooped figure of a man struggled for a moment to keep his balance on legs that seemed not to know quite how to handle the weight of his wasted body. Those nearest him moved to support him but were motioned back in a firm but kindly manner by anothe—a Rabbi perhaps—at whose encouragement the frail, warped figure began to straighten, unsteadily at first and then with more assurance. Now he raised his eyes from the ground and Timothy knew that he could never forget the mingled wonder and joy he saw there. The man put back his head and flexed his gaunt shoulders. Against his companions he was a small man but as he straightened now he seemed to rise above them.

Timothy, who had always regarded his own legs with disdain because of their puny size, knew a moment of guilt as he watched the pride and wonder with which this man put one foot before the other as he found he could indeed walk. Fascinated, Timothy watched the wasted figure walk slowly back and forth for a moment as though his legs were new and wonderful tools. Finally he fell upon his knees before the Rabbi, who helped him gently to his feet again.

Now a mother brought her baby. Its small body was covered with sores. A blind youth, led by the hand, groped his way. Several men half carried another who seemed possessed by a demon. There was a child with a large hump on his back; a cripple crawled on his knees. Was there no end to this stream of afflicted people? A woman with tears streaming down her face was dragging a badly deformed foot, a child burning with fever, a young girl with a withered hand—these and many more were brought before this calm, compassionate man who was surely more than a rabbi, for when He placed His hands upon their heads and blessed them, each one who had been afflicted came away rejoicing, whole and healed!

Watching in wonder and excitement, Timothy told himself that this must be the Nazarene of whom his father and uncles had spoken, the man who wrought miracles and taught a doctrine that was different from that taught by other rabbis. He had first heard of Him when his uncle returned from one of the special feast days in Jerusalem. He had listened spellbound while Uncle Ben described this young Galilean who had driven the astonished merchants and money changers from the temple with power and authority, saying, "Make not my Father's house an house of merchandise."

Now, as he realized the power of this man, whom His disciples called Jesus, Timothy's first thought was of his own grief. Surely one who could make whole the maimed and wretched could give unto another broad shoulders and strong limbs that a father might know joy in a stalwart son. As he watched the miserable people come and sensed the extent of their afflictions, his own problems dwindled, because he saw that he was blessed indeed to have seen the light of day and to walk without pain. When at length there were no more sick to bring, the multitude stayed as though they expected something more. One of the disciples rose and addressed the group. He spoke with dignity but also with some agitation. "The Master is exceedingly weary from long days of teaching and healing the sick among you. He has crossed over to this desert place only to have a few hours of solitude and rest. This ye have denied Him."

Timothy observed that the man seemed to be a Galilean fisherman not unlike his father. He was gently rebuked.

"Do not chide them, Peter. Hast thou not observed that they, too, are weary? They have walked a long distance around the shore with their sick and lame. Many are sick in spirit and hungry for the word of God. My heart is filled with compassion for them."

Then the Master turned upon the multitude. His countenance was beautiful. It was kind and gentle and understanding, yet lacking nothing in strength and dignity. The noise and din faded away, and the great sea of people waited to hear. No wonder Peter had called Him "the Master."

"Blessed are they who do hunger and thirst after righteousness for they shall be filled with the Holy Spirit."

Timothy sat upon the ground. He dropped his basket between his legs and straightway forgot everything save this man who spoke of the wondrous Kingdom of God as though He knew it personally. He spoke of it as though even Timothy and all that great multitude might come to know it. Indeed, as He spoke, the kingdom seemed not so distant. He likened it to seeds sown into the earth, to a treasure hid up in a field, to the net of the fisherman cast into the sea. But most surprising of all, He likened the kingdom of God to the sheep fold, guarded and protected by the Good Shepherd. He said, "I am the Good Shepherd. The Good Shepherd giveth His life for the sheep."

He spoke of the fishing nets, but He did not say, "I am the great fisherman." He spoke of treasures and fields, but He said, "I am the Good Shepherd."

He spoke of familiar things that were a part of the life Timothy knew, of patches on garments, of leavening and meal, of mustard seed, of houses and candles. He said, "It is more blessed to give than to receive." The boy found himself dwelling upon this thought. He remembered a handful of lilies he had taken to his mother and the glow he had felt inside at her joy in his thoughtfulness. He thought about the strange gourds he had found last season and painted with the juice of wild berries. The dried seeds inside had made a rattling sound when he shook them. How his younger brother Samuel had longed to have them in his hands for only a moment. He had wanted to give them to Samuel, to watch the delight and wonder in his face as he shook them. But, as he moved to do so, a bitter jealousy had come upon him. Samuel wanted everything! To him would go his very birthright, the honor and pride of sharing his father's work on the fishing boat.

In anger he had smashed the bright gourds before Samuel could so much as touch them. He remembered that he felt no feeling of gladness then, only the surprise and hurt in his little brother's eyes. It must be even as the Master said, more blessed to give than to receive. He had an overwhelming desire to experience the blessing of giving. He would find more gourds for Samuel, the small shells he kept in his pouch would please his sisters. More than anything, he wished that he had some very choice possession, a gift worthy to give to the Master Himself. Then, indeed could he know the joy of giving! What would please a man so great and wise? How could one such as he hope to obtain a gift of such worth?

So intently did he ponder, that he was not aware that the Master had finished speaking. It was a rude awakening to realize that the twilight hour was almost upon them. His sheep must be taken to the fold. His mother would soon be waiting for him to come to the evening meal. All at once he became aware that he was very hungry. He had forgotten to eat the food his mother had sent with him. His hand fell upon the small basket and he looked about eagerly for some spot away from the eyes of the multitude where he might break the loaves and eat. But there was no such spot; people were everywhere. He wondered if they, too, were hungry. Surely they were far from home; yet they did not move to go, and they seemed surprisingly undisturbed by the lateness of the hour. Listening to fragments of their conversation, some in argument, others in earnest speculation, he learned that they were wondering if this were the Messiah of whom it was written would someday come.

Timothy weighed the possibility. He sought The Master's face and found Him talking earnestly with the men who accompanied Him. Did he hear them speak of food? Or did this gnawing in his stomach cause him to imagine that all people were concerned at this moment with eating? Perhaps the Master, Himself, was hungry. The thought disturbed Timothy. He contemplated the food in his basket. It was little enough for one small person who had not eaten since morning.

Several of the disciples turned now and went among the multitude. They seemed reluctant to do so. They were asking again and again if any person had brought food. It was true then. Their leader was hungry! The boy watched anxiously. Would not someone in so great a number have food for the evening meal—sufficient food to share and not be hungry? But there was no word or gesture to indicate that anyone had so much as a morsel.

The basket in Timothy's lap was hardly to be noticed. If he sat just so, with his cloak upon his knees, it could not be seen at all. Surely, no one could need this meager meal so much as he did. It had been early morning when he broke his fast with goat milk and bread. Looking back now, it seemed that several days had passed since he had eaten food, and the emptiness inside was painful.

He saw that some of the disciples were returning now to report. The gestures and shrug of their shoulders indicated the futility of their efforts. The Master's face looked so disappointed and sad that Timothy was overcome with shame. Already this great man had been denied rest and solitude. Now he, Timothy, would also deny Him food!

The last disciple was making his way to where Jesus conferred with others of the group. Frantically, the boy hurried to the disciple. His slight frame shook with excitement as he grasped the man's cloak.

"Oh, sir, here in my basket is food for the Master!"

The man's face was doubtful. "How much food, Lad?"

"Five loaves and two fishes, sir." The disciple smiled kindly at the child's eagerness.

"Five loaves and two fishes are not enough, child. Better that ye eat and are yourself filled."

The words smote Timothy. Shameful tears stung his eyes and his chin quivered in spite of his efforts to control it. He knew that the emptiness inside him was not hunger alone. Seeing the boy's

Now a mother brought her baby.
Its small body was covered with sores.

disappointment, the disciple put a kind hand on his shoulder and graciously took the basket before he turned to inquire of others.

Timothy's first impulse was to run from all the strange people, back across the slopes to the single fig tree where he could throw himself upon the ground and give way to the tears that were so near and the lump in his throat that he could not swallow. But he felt impelled to know the fate of his offering. Now that he had given it, he knew a great many fears. Perhaps he had been too bold. Was it possible that the disciple had been laughing at him? He knew that the meal was small for a man fully grown, and perhaps it was not the kind to which a great man was accustomed. He hoped the loaves had not become smashed, or the fishes broken, or that the sun's strong rays had not made them both stale. How he wished that he had not eaten the goat cheese, that the Master might savor its mellow goodness.

He moved close to where the great rabbi counseled with His disciples, and he could make out His earnest voice above the din:

"Whence, Philip, shall we buy bread that these may eat?"

Whence indeed? Timothy well knew that there was no place within miles where bread could be bought. And then he realized that the Master was not concerned with food for Himself but for that vast crowd of people. The folly of his small contribution made him forget his other fears.

The man Philip was saying hopelessly, "Two hundred pennyworth of bread is not sufficient for them that everyone of them may take a little."

Timothy's face burned, and he felt overcome with apprehension and dismay. The disciple who had taken Timothy's basket was now moving forward to present the pitifully small contribution. To men who spoke of two hundred pennyworth of bread, who sought food to fill this mighty sea of people, his five small loaves must seem ridiculous indeed. The disciple was speaking reluctantly, "There is a lad here which hath five barley loaves and two small fishes, but what are they among so many?"

Miserably, Timothy wished the earth would swallow him up, that he might not see the face of the Master as He rejected the small offering. But the Master did not scorn Timothy's gift. He accepted the basket with dignity and graciousness, as though it might contain two hundred pennyworth of bread and more. "It is well, Andrew. Have the men sit upon the grass in groups of fifty."

His face was radiant as He spread Timothy's linen cloth, laid out the food and solemnly blessed it. He blessed it as though it were a great feast.

The tightness Timothy had felt in his chest was gone now, and he found that he could swallow the lump. There was no room for fear or apprehension, only wonder. He saw each of the twelve men take portions and impart barley loaves and fishes to the many groups. Methodically they went among the people. No one was missed and no one lacked food. As though under a spell, the boy watched, unable to take his eyes from the scene before him—hungry faces, greedy faces, eager faces, grateful faces—big hands tearing bread, small frantic hands picking bones from the fish; every one eating. Some ate calmly, finding the meal satisfactory, others ate as though they had not been filled in many days and had no assurance of food tomorrow. He began counting the groups and had counted near to a hundred when he became aware of a gentle hand on his shoulder and looked up into the face of the Master, Himself.

"And thou, lad, who gave thy meal that these might not be hungry, have ye no longer a desire to eat?"

He had forgotten his hunger! The kind voice and understanding eyes gave Timothy courage to speak.

"There was not enough in my basket to feed this many people, Master, only to . . ." He looked at the ground while he searched for words that might be understood. "Thou knowest that I did not know nor do I comprehend yet how my small loaves and fishes are enough to feed all of these."

The Master was not annoyed at the boy's perplexity. His answer was simple yet so grave and meaningful that Timothy knew he would never forget.

"All things are possible to the Father, and all things are wonderful. Dost thou comprehend, my son, how from so small an egg comes the fish thy father takes from the sea that provided our meal this day? Dost thou understand the barley, how a few seeds put into the earth sprout and grow to make a bounteous harvest from which thy mother grinds the meal to make these loaves?"

Timothy shook his head. These things had not seemed before to be things of wonder.

"Or how," The Master continued, "another seed might grow to be a vine laden with grapes and yet another might become a mighty tree?"

"Or a small fig tree!" Timothy had often wondered at the figs. "Yesterday they were small lumps on the branches. Now they have grown to the size of my thumb, and in a short time they will be plump and soft and very sweet to taste!"

The Master nodded, and Timothy understood that to Him the fig was a thing of wonder too. Perhaps He also liked to break the small seeds with His teeth.

"Who will say, Timothy, if these are not greater miracles than that which thou hast seen Me do today? Remember that all things are wonderful, and all things are possible with the Father. And among His wonders, nothing is greater than the lad who grows in stature and—more to be desired—in understanding. There is a strength that is greater than the strength of limb and body. It is an inner strength, born of the spirit, a strength that might cause a lad to care for an old ewe with an injured leg, or little orphaned lambs. A strength that might cause a hungry lad to give his own food that someone else might not be hungry."

The boy lowered his eyes and dug his toes into the ground.

"I gave so little food, only enough for one—it was in my heart to . . ."

"To give all one has, Timothy, is great in the sight of the Father, whether it be five loaves of barley or a great treasure." Then softly, but with so much love in His voice that Timothy raised his eyes to see that it was really himself to whom the Master spoke, "Or whether it be a cherished dream in a small boy's heart!"

The lump was in Timothy's throat again, but the awful emptiness was gone. His gifts were truly acceptable. The Master was smiling, and in his eyes was the joy he had seen in his father's eyes when he looked upon Samuel—all this for Timothy!—as though he were indeed a son to gladden the heart!

THE GOOD SHEPHERD

He said, "I am the Good Shepherd.
I know my sheep and my sheep know me.
They hear my voice and respond to my call
Wherever they may be."

"Though the way ahead be stormy,
Though the path be long and hard,
They know I watch and guide them:
Their Savior and their Lord!"

"I am the Good Shepherd."
He said it once more.
"I lay down my life for my sheep.
In giving my life, I open the door
For all the Father's children
To life forever more!"

"No man taketh my life from me.
Mine is the power to give,
Mine, also the power to take it again,
That every soul might live!"

Part 2

Timothy climbed the stairway to the roof and spread his mat to sleep. The air was crisp and cool now, and the stars shone brightly. Not in his eleven years did he remember having been permitted to stay awake so late, but there had never been a day such as this one before.

It was good to be alone now in the quiet of the night. He was comfortable with solitude and his own reflections. Tonight there was much to reflect upon. He must ponder on the Master's words to him. He wondered why his father and uncles had been so interested in his account of the Master. He had anticipated a satisfaction in telling them something of sufficient interest to cause them to raise their eyes from their food and listen, but had been quite unprepared for the intensity of their questions, the disputations among themselves over this man—whether indeed he might be the Messiah.

Joseph, the younger of the uncles, was sure that this soft-spoken man who concerned himself with the sick and maimed and with children could not have strength to break the bands of the Roman rule and restore Judea to her rightful place with God and man. But his uncle Ben had seen the money changers and the vendors cower before one man who had stood in power and authority before them and the unapproving priests and Pharisees as well. Timothy was sure there was nothing the Master could not do if he desired to do it.

Timothy had scarcely closed his eyes in sleep when he became aware that the day was breaking. It was yet dark but there were unmistakable noises and smells of early morning. His

"And thou, lad, who gave thy meal that these might not be hungry, have ye no longer a desire to eat?"

grandmother, Sarah, would be building a fire in the brick stove. Soon he would smell the rich aroma of roasting fish. He pulled his cloak closer around him against the early morning air and would have gladly given way to the drowsiness that pressed in upon him. Then, just as it would overpower him completely, he remembered that he had eaten with the men. They had listened to him and questioned him with respect. If he were to be one of them, he must, without being called, rise as did they, and be about the day's activities.

He took up his mat and, shivering, made his way down the ladder. He was glad for the small fire inside. His grandmother was fanning the glow. At the sight of him she grunted in mock disapproval, "Humph! This child has outgrown the need for sleep. He hears a rabbi speak, keeps us up late to tell us, then he is up again before the day begins."

His mother smiled fondly, "My son must keep pace with the men of the house and so must rise before his father." The slight child with his eager desire for acceptance was dear to her heart.

"Who must rise before his father?" A jovial voice filled the room, and a large frame filled the doorway. "This spindle-legged babe who but yesterday I carried on my shoulder?"

Timothy knew that his father's eyes sparkled in jest. But in spite of the jovial note in his father's voice, he tensed. He had not dared confront his father before, but now, remembering the wretched cripples he had seen the Master heal, he rose to his greatest height and said with all the dignity he could muster, "Nay, Father, let not my limbs be called spindles. My legs carry me whither I will, and my arms can do whatever work they are required to do."

The man sobered at the intensity of his son's words. Was there a shade of bitterness in his voice, or was it something of a plea? Surely the boy had not brooded all these years over this manner of referring to his frail limbs? A feeling of tenderness and remorse came over him, and he fought back an impulse to gather up the child in his arms and reassure him. Instead, he spoke with grave sincerity and respect. "My son is right. His limbs do serve him well and only with the coming of the spring grass have I noticed that his shoulders are becoming broader and his arms are growing in sinew."

Timothy flushed with pleasure at his father's words. Sensing his emotion, his grandmother brusquely turned the talk to the needs of the hour. "How is it that the sun is ready to show its face and there is yet no milk from the goat? Are we to talk while others catch all the fish in the sea and while the sheep stay penned in the fold?"

"My mother exaggerates our slothfulness," said Benjamin, laughing as he entered with a jar of milk. "Already is the brown goat milked and Joseph prepares the nets that we may catch our portion of the fish in the sea."

The merriment of their laughter brought Samuel from his mat. Hurrying to his father, he asked. "Will there be fish today, my father, or in truth is someone else catching all the fish in the Galilee as my grandmother has said?"

Simon laid a reassuring hand on his small son's head. "There will always be fish in the sea of Galilee." He then broke a barley loaf and all were silent while he blessed the food and opened the day with prayer.

As the men began their breakfast of warm brown fish and bread and curds, Simon spoke thoughtfully. "It is in my mind that perhaps it were well to let our neighbors have the fish from the sea today. I would listen to the words of the Nazarene while he is yet among us."

The men stopped eating. Sarah put down the fan and rose from the coals. Rachel looked up from the baskets of food she was preparing. Benjamin was first to speak.

"You would lose the day's catch?"

"There will always be fish in the sea of Galilee," Simon repeated with finality.

"Not in all the days since you came to this house do I remember a time when you were not first on the fishing boat in the morning!" Joseph's voice was unapproving. "Even before our father's death you took the responsibility. What is there in this rabbi that should take you from the work that sustains us?"

Sarah spoke now with the wisdom and dignity of her years. "It is true, Joseph. There has been little time save the Sabbath only when Simon has not been found at his work. Has he not earned a day to do with as he sees fit?"

Joseph dropped his gaze and mumbled, "My brother is a man and entitled to spend his day as he chooses."

There was silence for a moment, and then Benjamin spoke. "I respect my brother for his wisdom and his industry, but has he forgotten? This rabbi of Nazareth antagonizes the Pharisees. We hear rumors that they already seek reason to lay hands upon him!" He searched Simon's face with no little concern.

"I have forgotten nothing, Benjamin," Simon spoke gravely. "This night 1 have slept but little. 1 cannot be content to hear only rumors. Our fathers, our very prophets have foretold a Messiah since the beginning of time. Even the Pharisees, whose hypocrisies cause them to condemn this man, look for a deliverer. He has spoken in the synagogues in Capernaum, and only a few days ago his disciples were teaching in the villages. 1 would hear this rabbi with my own ears, even as my son Timothy heard him." He paused and then asked kindly, "Will my brothers come with me, or will they tend the fishing nets and continue to wonder?"

Joseph, still resentful, spoke with sharpness, "And be as others who already have left their boats to follow this man? Zebedee now must do the work of three. His two sons, along with Simon Bar Jonah and his brother no longer work with fishes and nets but follow this Nazarene. If Israel is to be saved from the yoke of Rome, it will be by someone worthy of the Royal House of David, not by the son of a poor carpenter of Nazareth whose very life is now in jeopardy. One of his disciples, called the Baptist, has already been beheaded."

Timothy's heart filled with fear. "Oh, Father, will harm come to the Master?"

Simon put his arm around the boy. "I think not, my son."

Timothy was thoughtful. "The Master said, 'I am the Good Shepherd. The Good Shepherd giveth his life for his sheep.' What did he mean, Father?"

"This I do not know, Timothy. Perhaps if I can but hear him I will better understand."

Sitting under the fig tree on the hillside, Timothy pondered the words of the Master, glad that his father would also hear. Was it true that the Pharisees were seeking to lay hands on him? Who was the Baptist who had been beheaded? Would they also harm his beloved Master? He could hardly wait for the evening to put the sheep in their fold. He must know of his father's experience.

He found his mother, Rachel, helping sisters Martha and Lydia with the evening meal. Where was Simon? The uncles seemed concerned. "It is said that this Rabbi went from Bethsaida to Capernaum. Perhaps Simon has followed him there."

"We will lose him again to the rabble-rousers! Judas, also, was from Galilee. This time Simon may not escape. He may even bring disaster to this house!"

Timothy turned to his mother. "What can they mean—disaster and rabble-rousers?" Before she could answer, Simon himself spoke from the doorway. "Your uncles speak in haste." Then addressing the men calmly but gravely he said, "There have, indeed, been uprisings. But know that Judas of Galilee was not a rabble-rouser nor a brigand. He was a true patriot. He feared God and not man." Simon spoke with stern conviction, "I was honored to be a follower of Judas of Galilee. He taught from the Torah and fought to free us from the cruel census and to restore the glory of Israel. He gave his life in this cause—I was not so faithful to it."

"But he is dead! The glory of Israel is not restored and you might have been crucified with two thousand others!" Joseph spoke with emotion. "This carpenter's son may even have helped build the crosses that Varus used to execute Judas and his followers."

Ben shook his head, "I shall never forget the sight of all those crosses over the hill at Sepphoris, nor the stench that hovered over the land. I shall not forget the terror in your face, Simon, when you stumbled to our boat on an evening as we drew in the day's fish. You were near dead from starvation and exhaustion."

Bursting into tears, Timothy ran to his father's side.

Sarah rose from her cooking, "We have avoided speaking of these things. They are to be forgotten! Simon is one of us. He has fulfilled the duties of this household since your father's death. Your sister is his wife and the mother of his children. Must they be frightened while you harass their husband and father?"

Simon put an arm around Timothy's frail shoulders, "It is now time to speak. True, I did consider Judas of Galilee to be a great leader and deliverer. Many good men followed him. It was a cruel awakening when Varus swept through the land with his legions of Roman troops. I did not fight bravely to the end as did many, but ran into the desert of Geneseret and hid myself. After days of hunger and exhaustion, I dared to go to your boat that evening. I sought only a little food, no more. I had watched your father, Joshua, with his two young boys. I knew he would not turn me over to the Roman soldiers. I knew too that protecting me might bring punishment. You have all been kind to me, regardless of danger. In this very house I was nourished and restored to health. Joshua became my father, Ben and Joseph, my brothers. Sarah has been my mother, and Rachel, my blessed wife. Here my children have been born and nurtured. I am grateful and would not cause you anxiety. Tomorrow I shall be with you and the nets on the Galilee, but I shall hide myself no longer. I will have my turn in carrying fish to the markets of Capernaum

There is none who could take from Me My life.
It is Mine to give in love—
A part of His plan of happiness,
Designed by the Father above!

and Bethsaida. I must hear again the words of this rabbi and learn if he be the Messiah we seek."

"Your zeal in seeking the Messiah has brought you trouble."

"Yes, Joseph, I once felt that the cause of Israel could be won by superior strength and the sword. I am now feeling that the Messiah will not come with an army. This man speaks of a kingdom that is not of this world. Today he chastened the multitude who followed him only to eat bread. He offers 'the Bread of Life.' He said, 'I am the Bread of Life; He that cometh to me shall never hunger, and he that believeth in me shall never thirst.'"

"Is it not ridiculous to believe that one might never be hungry or thirsty?"

Simon was patient. "Joseph, my brother, like the multitude, you think in terms of bread and fishes. The Master said, 'Verily, I say unto you, he that believeth in me hath everlasting life.' I do not understand all, but I am drawn to him. I will hear more."

Timothy's love for his father had never been greater. He wondered why they found it so much easier to talk together than ever before.

The springtime turned into summer. Timothy was glad for figs that ripened and for the two new baby lambs from the ewe. No longer did he feel that he must hide his love for the sheep. Again and again he remembered the Master's words, "I am the good shepherd."

His father and uncles spoke often of rumors they heard at the market places. Many people had been healed: the blind, the lame, the demoniac. Timothy did not wonder at this. It was even said that a dead man was restored to life. Even so, many who once sought the Master no longer followed the Nazarene. He was said to eat with common hands, not following the ceremonial washings. He disregarded many rites and customs. He healed on the Sabbath. He ate with sinners. Joseph felt that the disapproval of the Pharisees would soon result in his arrest. Ben still remembered the cleansing of the temple and was sure that when the time came, this Rabbi would show his great power and bring Israel to her rightful place. Simon spoke little, but as the rains began again and the grass turned green, he talked of attending the Passover in Jerusalem. He was firm in his decision. It had been years since he had attended a Passover celebration in Jerusalem.

"My son is now twelve years of age and on the threshold of manhood. I would have him and his mother see the City of David and the holy temple with me. Perhaps we shall see the Master and again hear his words."

The joy and anticipation were almost more than Timothy could bear. He shed tears as he explained to the first born and choicest of the lambs that it was an honor to be offered as a sacrifice at the temple. They must arrive several days early to make arrangements.

Neither Rachel nor Joseph had been to Jerusalem, and though Ben had made the pilgrimage three years earlier, he longed to return. It was decided to let the fishing boats rest and leave the children and animals in Sarah's charge. The girls, now in their eighth and tenth years were quite capable of tending the sheep.

They traveled on foot with other families from Geneseret. Rachel joined with the women. She had baked loaves for the journey. They carried curds, roasted fish, honey, and dates. At night they set up camp, the men taking turns to guard against brigands and highwaymen. Timothy was never far from his father's side.

At last they reached the crest of the ridge of hills at the north of the city. Timothy had been taught the traditions and history of the Jews. He knew about the great city and the temple but he was not prepared for this sight. Before them lay the great sprawling metropolis, shining palaces, public buildings, high strong walls, stands and booths of tradesmen, narrow streets thronging with people—and above all, the temple, its walls gleaming like snow on the mountain top.

The travelers from Galilee were weary—glad to rest, to prepare for purification, and to make arrangements to sacrifice the paschal lamb. Timothy was his father's shadow. He listened as the men speculated about this Jesus of Galilee—a man from their own place.

Accustomed to the disdain of the ruling class, they reveled in the attention this Galilean received. Could he really be the Messiah? Would he declare himself and bring the hosts of heaven to his aid? While resting, Timothy, ever close to his father's side, listened to them speak of rumors and events. The Pharisees had abandoned their prejudices and joined with other ruling classes, even the Herodians. It was said that they had sent spies, feigning themselves to be just men seeking his wisdom—this to trap and deliver him to the power of the government.

"Master," they said, "We know that thou art true and teachest the way of God. Tell us therefore, what thinkest thou? Is it lawful to give tribute to Caesar or not?"

Jesus had perceived their trap and asked to see the tribute money. "Whose is the image and superscription?"

They answered, "Caesar's."

"Render then unto Caesar the things that are Caesar's and to God the things that are God's."

As they spoke, they marveled at his wisdom. "Surely he will out-wit those who would take his life."

"Their frenzy at his power has been doubled. They are more incensed than ever because he raised a dead man to life in Bethany—he was dead for four days!"

Simon was pensive. "I would see this man who was dead and is alive." He looked into Timothy's eager face. "On the morrow we go to Bethany."

Others too were drawn to see. The multitude gathered around the home of Simon, the Leper, where a supper was being prepared for Jesus and the twelve. Martha, a sister of Lazarus (the man who had been dead), was in charge of the meal.

Lazarus sat at the table with Jesus who was teaching. Jesus spoke of the Kingdom of Heaven—that is like a tiny grain of mustard seed, which put into the ground, sprouts and grows to be a tree in which the birds nest. He spoke of the sheepfold: "I am the Good Shepherd and know my sheep and am known of mine. As the Father knoweth me, even so I know the Father; and lay down my life for the sheep."

Timothy remembered the teachings on the hillside. He had wondered about these words, and now the Master was explaining.

"Therefore doth my Father love me, because I lay down my life that I may take it up again. No man taketh it from me, but I lay it down of myself. I have power to lay it down and I have power to take it again. This commandment have I received from my Father."

With the simple faith of a child who had seen the Master's works, Timothy would remember these words again and again in the days ahead when they returned to Jerusalem.

The multitude lay palm leaves and spread their cloaks for the Master as He rode on a colt. Many, shouting "HOSANNA," were sure that Jesus would now rise up, bring down the heavenly hosts and redeem Israel! Timothy knew this would not be. The Master had said that the kingdom of heaven would sprout and grow with time.

As Timothy witnessed many turning against the Master, reviling and spitting upon Him, and beating and crucifying Him, he wept bitter tears. He felt as though his heart would break that his beloved Master must suffer so. But he remembered:

"I lay down My life for *the sheep.*
No man taketh it from Me.
I have power to lay it down
And to *take it up again.*"

He was filled with joy, but not astonishment, when women who had traveled with them from Geneseret came running to tell them that the tomb was found empty and an angel had declared, "*He is not here, but he is risen and will go before ye into Galilee*!"

The beloved Master, who had accepted his small gift of loaves and fishes and fed a multitude with it, gave His life, and with that solitary gift, multitudes would enter into His kingdom!

"There is none who could take from Me My life,
It is Mine to give in love—
A part of His plan of happiness,
Designed by the Father above!"

REFERENCES: PART I

Matthew 14:13–21
Mark 6:31–44
Luke 9:10–17
John 6:1–14

Jesus and His Times

Reader's Digest Association, pages 237, 238, and 240. Published in the United States of America, fourth printing, July 1990.

REFERENCES: PART II

John 10:11, 14, 15, 17, 18
John 12:1–12
Matthew 22:15–21
Mark 12:12–17
Luke 20:20–25

Jesus and His Times

Reader's Digest Association, pages 204–7.

Josephus

Antiquities of the Jews, book 17, chapter 10, section 5, 8, and 10.

The Bible Almanac

Guideposts, Carmel N.Y., page 509
Acts 5: 37

Direct quotations are from the Bible only. The other books were studied for background and information.

About the Author

Naomi Stevens Smith was born October 22, 1914. Her parents had left the Mormon colonies in Chihuahua, Mexico, during the time of Pancho Villa, so she was born in El Paso, Texas, as a citizen of the United States.

As the eldest of eleven children and eventually the mother of eight, the demand for stories began early in her life. Over the years she has printed special stories for families, but *Something to Give* is her first published work.

Naomi spent much of her childhood and youth in Colonia Juarez, Mexico, and in the little mountain town of Colonia Chuichupa. She graduated from the Juarez Stake Academy and was among the first group of LDS missionaries called to serve in Mexico when that country was reopened for missionary work after being closed to proselyting by the government for approximately twenty years.

She later attended Brigham Young University, where she met and married Don Hyrum Smith in 1940. They enjoyed twenty-five happy years together with their children before his accidental death in 1965.

Naomi taught school in Salt Lake City's Granite School District for fifteen years, and then filled a Spanish-speaking mission for the LDS Church to Mexico and Arcadia, California.

At present she resides in Salt Lake City and enjoys teaching an English class to Spanish-speaking friends, gardening, community and church service. She also enjoys being with her large and loving family, which includes forty-five grandchildren and many greatgrandchildren, with more arriving all the time.